Elements Journal

Janet E. Lapp, RN, PhD

Library of Congress Publisher's Cataloging In Publication Data
Lapp, Janet E.
Four Elements of Transformation Journal

Janet E. Lapp
p.cm.
Includes bibliographic references and index.

Print: ISBN 1-885365-78-0

1. Self-actualization (psychology) 2. Change (psychology)
3. Leadership
I.Title II. Title:
BF637.S4S24 2002
158' . 1-
dc20

Journal Contents

How to Use your Journal

Although the exercises and guidelines in the Journal can stand alone, they will make sense if used in conjunction with the book: *The Four Elements of Transformation.* Reference is made in *The Four Elements* to exercises, and are timed to be completed in a certain order.

Each section contains suggestions for nutrients to support your body and mind while developing the skills and attitudes in each Element. Only information that is research-based and empirically derived has been used. Suggestions are made for aromas, herbs, and colors that will enhance each Element. Research on these factors is anecdotal and incomplete, but I have tried to give you the most helpful information I could find. None of these substances substitute for needed medical care. If you are experiencing symptoms that interfere with your quality of life, please consult a physician, physician's assistant or nurse practitioner.

At the beginning of each element is a meditation to repeat throughout your work with that Element. For the Earth Element, for example, it is "I am aware and awake, knowing and owning my true purpose." There are Four Elements Meditation Cards available that can assist you.

Each Element will take about 10 days to complete, depending on how much time you have to devote. Travel at your own pace. If you work diligently, you can complete your transformation work in about 40 days (you can speed through the whole system in a few days!). As you cycle up in awareness and practice, you will return to your Four Elements System for additional growth.

Join the Four Elements System at my website www.lapp.com so you can call in to our regular teleseminars for encouragement and support.

FOUR ELEMENTS JOURNAL
ELEMENT ONE: EARTH

Voice your intention. With your eyes, trace from left up the side of the structure above, down the right, across the bottom, then repeat: "I am aware and awake, knowing and owning my true purpose."

There are several associations with the Earth Element: The compass direction North, the autumn season, older age, the colors brown and green, feminine energy, strength, stability and abundance.

Some of the work toward the end of each element will incorporate these attributions, but our purpose here is to create the foundational basis for your transformation. That basis is to create the stability that results from accountability, responsibility and authenticity. To know yourself, own your gifts, and express your truth.

CORE QUESTIONS

If you feel you are not expressing what it is that you want to do or were meant to do, begin by considering these first questions. If you get stuck, keep moving and come back later.

1. If there were something different or unique about you, what would it be?

2. What do people say about you? How do they describe you? If you don't know, ask them. You're missing out on valuable information. Ask your friends what they think is your natural talent and write it here:

3. What part of your work/life do you love?

4. What part of your work/life isn't much fun?

Write a short, meaningful and convincing statement about what you do. Memorize it, and repeat it to yourself several times a day. This is ***not*** an 'elevator promo.' Rather, it is to convince *you* that your mission is worthwhile and meaningful. It might sound something like, "I allow others to connect with me such that they sense my strength and courage, and thus feel encouraged, hopeful and optimistic about their own lives."

Repeat this until the committee in your head that argues with it, doubts it, and denies it, is silent. **Write it here:**

Draw Toward your Life

The purpose of this exercise is to begin to draw your life toward what it was meant to express. Roll tape on your life as it appears five years from now and as you would like it to be.[1] When you can let your video run for a few minutes without extinguishing it with your 'dampeners' or self-put-downs that you use–or, the 'committee-in-your-head' – you will start to detach fear from the video and attach calm. That will help draw you toward it.

Write down what you would really love to do, no holds barred:

Someday I'd really love to:

If I could, I would:

I've always wanted to:

Wouldn't it be super if:

1 More on this in Part II: Water Element. This is preliminary work.

What are your answers? Think they're unrealistic? They're not. Haven't others done similar things? Why not you?

"DO WHAT ONLY YOU CAN DO AND DO IT SO WELL THAT PEOPLE WILL COME FROM ALL OVER TO SEE YOU DO IT."

Hang on to these statements throughout the first Element. You would not be thinking about these statements if they weren't meant for you.

MORE CORE QUESTIONS

These Core Questions will take you deeper into personal meaning. Take the time to think about them, because your answers will guide you to your strengths and to your barriers. My personal responses follow each question as a prompt and suggestion.

My examples are short and meant to be illustrative. Make yours as lengthy as you can or want. Some of my coaching clients have written pages for each question, and have found their truth becoming more and more transparent to them as they wrote. I encourage you to engage in writing as a daily practice.

1. What do you wish your parents had known that would have made things easier or better for them?
I wish my parents had known about good communication, and about mental health.

2. How has that wish or perceived lack, evolved into a strength or a talent for you?
I've worked hard to learn communication and to study mental health.

3. What impact did the way your parents grew up have on you? What lessons or beliefs did they impart from their time?
My parents were born when there were restrictions on women and unbalanced power of men. There was a market crash and depression in the 1930's. They transmitted fears and cautions. The Second World War led to more uncertainty. They were cautious, afraid that "something would happen" because it always did.

4. What do you wish your parents had known about life that you know now? *I wish they had know that openness, not secrecy led to the truth, and that the truth would always rise no matter what. In those days, the family*

façade was protected by secrecy; there is much that we could not talk about. So we quietly bore it, doubting ourselves, not know what was normal and what wasn't.

5. What did you miss most in your childhood? If there was something you could go back and experience differently, what would it be?

Everything that was on my path led me to exactly where I am now, and I know I am supposed to be here. So if I experienced differently, I would be different now. Having said that, I missed a family, a feeling of safety and closeness.

6. Is there anything you would do differently for your own children, or perhaps your grandchildren?

I am being more open, active, honest, involved. Emotionally available.

7. Is there any guidance that would have helped you when you were a teen? If you could share that advice with teens now, what would you tell them? How would you want it to change their lives?

It would have helped to know that my feelings were a normal reaction to a strange world, rather than believing that they were a strange reaction to a normal world.

8. What do you love to do that adds value to the lives of others or makes our world a better place? What kind of impact would you like to have on other people's lives? What is the most profound impact you would like someone to experience as a result of what you are doing or want to do?

My career has allowed me to reach thousands of people. I want to give others permission (to act, to be, to move), to un-label themselves, and show them the steps to a successful and fulfilled life.

9. What do you value most about yourself–what do you like the most, are you most proud of? This is

probably the same quality you admire most in others, and a quality held by your favorite son or daughter. *Resilience, perseverance.*

10. Do you know your shadow? What annoys you most about others? What quality bothers you about your least favorite son or daughter? *Focus on self.*

Look over these pages at what you've written. Whenever you read something that provokes or stirs you, ask yourself: "Why is this important to me? How has this influenced me? Is this important right now?" Complete the statements below.

I feel it's important to:

I feel at my best when:

I want my life to be more:

My biggest wish I have is to live my life:

The purpose of my life is to:

EXCUSES

a. On the form below, rank your perceived success out of 10 in each area of your life. Include the following areas; financial, emotional, family, friends, spiritual, creative, health, career, and fitness. The rating of 10 doesn't represent societal standards, it represents *your* standards. It represents what *you* would find satisfying and joyful in life.

RANK YOUR SUCCESS

FINANCIAL	1	2	3	4	5	6	7	8	9	10
EMOTIONAL	1	2	3	4	5	6	7	8	9	10
FAMILY	1	2	3	4	5	6	7	8	9	10
FRIENDS	1	2	3	4	5	6	7	8	9	10
SPIRITUAL	1	2	3	4	5	6	7	8	9	10
CREATIVE	1	2	3	4	5	6	7	8	9	10
HEALTH	1	2	3	4	5	6	7	8	9	10
CAREER	1	2	3	4	5	6	7	8	9	10
FITNESS	1	2	3	4	5	6	7	8	9	10

b. Then list what you need to do to bring each area to a '10.' As you enter what you need to do to upgrade each area from a seven to a ten, two elements appear: the reasons you have been using to prevent you from being a 10, and the very next steps you need to take to get there.

The question follows: if you *know* what needs to be done, why aren't you doing it? The answers that you give will indicate your fears, with some disguised as excuses. If you are aware of what needs to be done, of what *can* be done, then you have the capacity to do it.

List what you need to do to bring each area to a 10.

FINANCIAL

EMOTIONAL

FAMILY

FRIENDS

SPIRITUAL

CREATIVE

HEALTH

CAREER

FITNESS

Don't wait for permission to do what you want to do. There will always be excuses. Take the leap, and list what it would take to make each area 10. Why not upgrade everything you are doing into a 10 out of 10. If you settle for mediocrity or 'good enough' in one area of your life, it will spread out into other areas where you really *do* want to be excellent.

EXCUSES EXERCISE

If you have heard yourself use excuses, or hear them from those around you, here is a simple exercise:

a. Choose one big thing you could do that would make a huge impact on your life, that you are not now doing.

Write it here:

b. Why are you not doing it? Do any of these familiar excuses come up?

“I can't afford it.”

“I have nothing original to say.”

“It's all been said before.”

“I don’t have the confidence.”

“I would never make it.”

“My kids are too young.”

“He’s so much better at it than me.”

“I'm too (old, fat, ugly, short).”

“I don't have time.”

“I don't want to bother people.”

“ ______________________________.”

What role do each of these excuses–or others–play in your life? What do they allow you to do? Do they protect you from failure? Write down what comes to mind next to the excuse.

Repeat each excuse and then say to yourself. “That is just an imagined excuse to protect myself from failure. If I keep it, I will fail. Don't go there. It's not true."

Face your Excuses

Some of these statements might stir up resentment from you. If a statement does that, consider it a gift of insight. The statement is touching a chord deeper than your awareness. If you can play that chord and get in touch with the truth, then you can be freed of its constriction around you.

I'll be happy when ____________ and the reason I am not choosing this is: ____________.

If only I had ____________ and the reason I am not choosing this is: ____________

If I had more money, I could ____________ and the reason I am not choosing this is: ____________.

I would really be successful if I ____________ and the reason I am not choosing this is: ____________.

Someday I would really love to ____________ and the reason I am not choosing this is:____________.

People who have had the same excuses that you have, have done amazing things after they made the decision to **not allow themselves any excuses at all.**

You alone can decide whether or not you want to keep your excuses. One of the most powerful parts of your program is to never, never allow yourself any at all. And if you do uncover any, give yourself credit and advise yourself, "You developed this excuse because you needed it then. You don't need it any more. Gradually you will let it go."

CREATING THE EARTH ELEMENT

Throughout your work with the Earth Element, use the sensory resources in this section. To increase the your experience of discovery of purpose and meaning, and to accept responsibility, requires centering and calming.

This is the work of the first Element, to be completed before other elements can take hold in your life. Your environment, the food you eat, how you think, the people with whom you spend time–all matter. Choose well.

AROMATHERAPY

- [ ] **Vanilla.** Everywhere.
- [ ] **Ginger:** is a warm scent with calming undertones.
- [ ] **Lemon:** Although lemon has energizing properties, it calms and has a cleansing effect after a space is cleared (either mentally or physically).
- [ ] **Chamomile:** The scent has soothing properties especially at bedtime. Pair it with lavender.
- [ ] **Sandalwood:** Sandalwood is used for meditative spaces; a warm and woody scent with lots of depth; pair it with rose.
- [ ] **Bergamot:** relaxing and soothing; sniffing it actually has a marked positive effect on slow

brainwaves. There is some evidence that it has an anti-depressant effect.[2]

- ☐ **Ylang ylang:** inspires a sense of calm and relaxation. Pair it with bergamot.
- ☐ **Lavender:** Use lavender as an essential oil. Trying growing your own lavender and drying it.

HERBS

Any of these products: alfalfa, barley, buckwheat, corn, cotton, cypress, fern, honeysuckle, magnolia, oats, patchouli, pea, potato, rye, sage, tulip, wheat–should be increased during your Earth Element work. No need for a garden. Working in earth is calming, so why not buy a planter and base, fill half up with potting soil, and plant a couple of herbs? Line the entrances of your home with **patchouli oil.** Hang a small **sage sachet** over windows and doors opening to the north.

NUTRIENTS

Increase Magnesium (Mg). Corporations don't earn as much from Magnesium (Mg) as they do from Calcium and other relentlessly-promoted products, so you won't hear much about it. Most of us don't get

---

2 There is no harm in adding these herbs or spices to your environment, and they *are* helpful. The harm is in expecting therapeutic relief. Treatment for clinical depression should be done with a trained healthcare professional.

the minimum RDA[3] for Mg and guess what? Lowered Mg levels can lead to a feeling of unrest, anxiety, and scatter. Contracted muscles and difficulty sleeping are both signs of possible Mg deficiency.

Eat magnesium-rich foods such as beans, nuts and vegetables and make sure your food contains some fat.[4] Switching to all low-fat food might be depriving you of needed fat to absorb antioxidants; and subjecting you to the additives put into the food to improve taste. Avoid obviously fried foods and empty, high glycemic foods. Anything bright pink or blue, cakes and cookies. Empty high calorie foods like candies, processed (not raw) chocolate, chips (doesn't matter how "natural" they make them sound), sodas, cookies and anything refined, fill you with empty calories, and are always low in Mg.

Keep calcium levels high, but make sure your Mg levels match. Don't drink lots of milk and pile in the calcium without taking Mg because Calcium is a

---

3 Recommended Daily Allowance–the minimum to sustain life.

4 A study reported in the American Journal of Clinical Nutrition stated that "No absorption of carotenoids was observed when salads with fat-free salad dressing were consumed. A greater absorption of carotenoids was seen when salads were eaten with full-fat than with a reduced-fat salad dressing."

magnesium antagonist. You think you are creating healthy bones when you might be hurting your heart.

Overdoing alcohol causes a loss of Mg. Many hangover symptoms such as headache, noise sensitivity, and light sensitivity, are the same as symptoms of Mg deficiency. Caffeine can lower Mg levels.
Mashed potatoes, banana smoothies, soy milk, home made vegetable broth, peanuts are all good sources. Peanuts are high in both Mg and fat, and the fat may make the Mg more absorbable. Cashews and pistachios, dark green vegetables, tuna, bananas, cashews, almonds, spinach, tomato paste are all good.

Click this link for Magnesium content of foods

- ❑ **Berries.** Eat slowly, one by one. Any berry will do. Also the vitamin C in them will counteract a rise in cortisol, a stress hormone.
- ❑ **Guacamole.** Avocados have lots of B vitamins, which stress depletes, and good fat you need to absorb other nutrients.
- ❑ **Nuts.** Walnuts add B vitamins, Brazil nuts add zinc, which anxiety depletes. Almonds boost E, which is a natural antioxidant.
- ❑ **Chai tea.** Make your own chai. A warm drink is soothing. Try aromatic decaf chai tea in ready-to-brew bags, buy the powder, or mix warm milk and chai.

- [ ] **Oranges.** Oranges are easy to carry around and boost Vitamin C levels another antioxidant.
- [ ] **Asparagus.** Each stalk is a source of folic acid, a natural mood lightener. Dip the spears in fat-free yogurt or sour cream for added calcium.

You have completed the exercises for Element One: The Earth Element. You have come a long way to defining yourself and your purpose. You have worked through your excuses and are heading toward an excuse-free life. You are adding nutritional and herbal elements to enhance your work. You're ready for Element Two: Water.

FOUR ELEMENTS JOURNAL

ELEMENT TWO: WATER

Face the blue element of water.
Let your eyes circle clockwise in
the morning and in the evening,
circle counter clockwise. Voice
your intention. "Thank you Water
for harmony, order, and focus."

Water was originally the 'Primordial Chaos', associated with dissolution, union and transformation, and with the goddess Persephone, who ruled over death and rebirth in the Underworld. Psychologically, water is likely to be the predominant element in people who tend to be flowing, flexible, and oriented toward harmony or union. Common attributions include: West, winter, youth, the colors blue, violet and gray, and feminine energy.

Formally, Water is the Element of Emotions and Relationships, and is the child of Air. This means the Mind is the basis for emotions. Water is the Element for all emotions and relationships, both positive and negative. Your intention for invoking Water is to help you improve your emotional state or relationships by unblocking or releasing restrictions. For our purposes, and paradoxically, this release will be accomplished by organization, focus, discipline and will. You will experience openness and flow in your career as well as personal life when you develop the skills in this Element.

LEARNING FOCUS

With time and careful observation, you might even be able to avoid the distraction altogether if you can dig into the trigger by paying attention to:

* Where you are
* What distracts you
* What time of day is it
* Who else is around
* How tired are you
* Your hunger level
* What emotion(s) you have

Here are more advanced statements to use when you are tempted, similar to the ones you used for distractions:

1. "What is the worst thing that could happen if I were to face this, if I were to stick with it?

2. "What is the best thing that could happen to me if I were to face this and continue with it?

3. "What would happen if I just kept avoiding it – what will my life be like if I do not change this, do not accomplish it?"

4. "What will I be like in five years if I avoid this, or if I quit?

Here's an example of what your responses might look like *(these are both mine).*

Problem: *Cannot complete book. Avoid writing.*
Base Fear: *Unsure about quality of book and its usefulness.*

* Where are you most likely to be?
At my computer in my office.
* What do you turn to?
The internet (random searches), naps, food
* What time of day is it? *Any time.*
* Who else is around? *Nobody.*
* How tired or alert are you? *Alert when sitting down and then very sleepy.*
* Hungry or feeling full? *Usually hungry.*
* What emotion(s) are you most likely feeling just before your distraction? *Boredom.*

Maximize Focus

1. Prepare. There is no substitute.
2. **Sleep!**
3. Work out. Everything counts. Keep moving.
4. Be still for 15 minutes. Clear your thinking.
5. Eat a well-balanced meal.

Quality of Actions

An assessment of Quality of Actions can create a higher awareness of what is paying off, and what isn't. Does the casual lunch with a long-standing client who loves you but will never give you more business, a high payoff activity? How about a round of golf with a CEO of a company who is currently doing business with a competitor? How about time spent on the internet wandering around various competitor's websites, or wandering around Facebook just in case? Watching TV? Making coffee? Do a 24-hr time-motion study on your current work-life activities, and you will find decision-making easier in the future.

Begin with the Core Truth that you developed in Element One–Earth Element. Using the above Quality of Activities form, find out what value your activities hold for you. Rate:

a. how **interesting** they are to you
b. the **value** they have in fulfilling your Core Truth
c. the **ease** with which you can fulfill them

At first, watch what you kinds of things you find yourself doing, and ask yourself if they line up with your Core Truth. Then, assign numbers to these events or objects according to the legend on the next page. Finally, make decisions about whether or not you still want the events or objects in your life, given the rankings that you have given them. After you calculate your activities for a couple of days, you will be able to make more automatic decisions on how to spend your time.

Let's take the first example on the form. Lunch - John. John is a long-standing client and a good guy. His office is near some good restaurants, so that's a 5 for least effort. You enjoy lunches with him (that rates a 4 for Fun). So multiply 5x4, the resulting ExF

ITEM	E x F	x V =	W	ACTION
John-lunch	5 X 4 = 20	X 1 =	20	Drop
CEO-golf	2 X 4 = 8	X 5 =	40	Keep

LEGEND

E = Effort or how much trouble or risk.

F = Fun. How satisfying is this during and afterwards. Is it enjoyable? Does it leave you feeling fulfilled?

V = Is this high value? Something that you have identified to be a long-term viable strategy for you? Does this move you toward your goals?

P = This is the Payoff factor. What's the real payoff for you, personally or professionally?

score is 20/25, which is good! Once a month or so, you go out to lunch with John, and charge it to your account.

Now, the only problem is that John's not going to give you any additional business, and doesn't value his lunches as much as you think he does. What he really needs from you, are ways in which he can grow his business. So the VALUE score is only about 1. Multiply 1x20 = 20. Scores can range from 1 to 125, so 15 is not even in the top half. You might want to continue lunches if you enjoy them, but maybe once a year; or monthly if you count it as social, personal time rather than business time, and don't charge your company.

It was some effort getting a round of golf with the CEO of a company whose business you want (hence the score of 2) but the fun factor was 4, so that is a score of 8. Not that high, but now multiply it by a Value Score of 5, you get a sum of 40. Not great, but twice the value of the lunch with John and as time goes by, the ease will increase to 5, and Fun will be 5, times 5 = 125, a top score. If no business results from the game, you will need to lower the Value Score. You make the cutoff where you decide to drop activities, or just use the form to rank your priorities and do them in order.

When you make decisions around your Core Truth, many items will naturally fall out, and many items might never get into your life. Decision-making will be easier. You have a right to these choices. There are no rules to follow except the law that holds you to your Truth. If your Core Truth is as simple as "I help others and enjoy my life," and someone is in your life who you don't enjoy[5], then make a decision about that person.

If your work duties are dictated for you, your company still needs you to carefully evaluate the worth that your current activities have toward the new vision of the company. Evaluate what you're currently doing – whether it is high payoff, if it can be automated, or if it needs to be done at all. Spend time on activities that you have decided are high payoff for your company. Some departments have held successful 'Dumb Rules Contests' to uncover outdated and unused policies and procedures, saving their company tons of money and time, and having fun in the process.

SOCRATIC REASONING

Here's an example of reasoning that helps to dig below the surface of limiting fears. Supposing a client (C) described a phobia of bridges. She cannot cross a bridge, no matter what. To make sure that I (T) am treating the correct problem, we engage in a

5 In a care-taking situation, where you are voluntarily looking after someone who cannot look after him or herself, then you are making a conscious decision about helping, and just need to find a part of your work joyful.

dialog similar to the one below. You might find it useful to use it to question your own resistance.

T: "What would happen if you crossed a bridge?"
C: "I don't know, I would ... die?
T: "Die?"
C: "Ok, maybe not die, but I would feel terrible, I would panic, my heart would race, I couldn't breath."
T: "Then what would happen?"
C: "Well, I might faint, or lose consciousness."
T: "Ok, and then what?"
C: "Well, I wouldn't know because I have lost consciousness."
T: "Ok, but what do you think would happen next?"
C: "Well, I suppose that someone would find me, and call for help."
T: "And then what would happen?"
C: "I would be taken somewhere and helped, and I guess feel better."
T: "Then how would that be, with you waking up and everybody around your bed?"
C: "I would feel embarrassed, ashamed of myself, weak." The client emotionally attaches to this statement. It is her feeling of shame and weakness that needs support, not her presenting symptom, phobia of bridges.

SCATTER QUIZ

Yes No

____ ____ Do you tend to go from one project to another without completing much?

____ ____ Do you tend to hoard things like papers, magazines, clippings, and never get around to using them?

____ ____ Do you have any clutter in your physical space?

____ ____ Are your finances in disarray - such that you do not always balance your checkbook, and are not sure of your net worth?

____ ____ Do you sometimes tend to forget things, let appointments slip by?

____ ____ Are there broken items around your house that need repair but you never seem to get around to them?

____ ____ Are you either late for appointments or find yourself rushing at the last minute to try to make them?

Add up the 'yes' check marks. If you checked 5 or more, please check the items below as well:

____ ____ Is your mood up and down?

____ ____ Do you consume more sugar and/or caffeine than you should?

____ ____ Do you drink more alcohol than you probably should?
____ ____ Depression or the 'blues' a problem?
____ ____ Any trouble sleeping?

Checked more than two?

Mood swings and substance use or overuse often go together. Using alcohol, sugar and caffeine to cope with moods and stress is just asking for more instability. Why not make a plan to get everything under control: lack of exercise, poor food habits, alcohol use. It's possible. What are you waiting for?

CLUTTER CHECK

> Clutter is chaos, and chaos brings more chaos, not abundance.

This part involves recognizing *how* you are cluttering, and getting back on track. Be patient, this is important work and has to be done. Once you do it and make a habit out of it, watch out for the good that will pour into your life!

What do you hoard/clutter/keep in chaos? Check below and add your own.

___ Reading materials, magazines? *Do you fear not knowing, not being smart?*

___ Finances? *Do you fear having, or not having enough money?*

___ Is your daily schedule cluttered? *Do you fear of not doing enough?*
___ Keeping old clothes? *Fear of not having enough money to buy more?*

Everything that does not carry your life forward, throw it out. Throw out magazines and newspapers. Start fresh with tomorrow's paper and next week's magazine.

List here what still needs to get into order:

1 ....
2 ....
3 ....

Get a friend to help you to begin clearing the stuff you collect around fear. It will be hard. But you absolutely need to do it.

For those items left over from your **Clearing Checklist** (on page 38), list what needs to get into order, and clean out one area a week, starting with the area of **highest payoff/lowest pain**.

Here's how that works: Create four columns. Enter the item name in the left column, for example, 'Desk junk drawer.' In column 2, rate the payoff for organizing it from 1 – the least payoff to 10 – the most payoff – let's say you rate the payoff a 6 out of

10. Then, rate the pain of doing it, with 1 – the most pain and 10 – the least pain. Supposing the pain is fairly high, for example a 3. Multiple 6x3=18, and enter that number in the far right column.

Supposing the next area is the magazine pile at the edge of your desk. In column 2, rate the payoff for eliminating the pile from 1 – the least payoff to 10, the most payoff – let's say you rate the payoff a 3 out of 10, not too high. Then, rate the pain of doing it, with 1 the most pain and 10 the least pain. Supposing the pain is fairly low, for example a 9. Multiple 3x9=27, and enter that number in the far right column.

After a few of these calculations you'll be able to order them from highest to lowest, thus getting the highest payoff with the lowest amount of pain.

ITEM	PAYOFF	PAIN	RANK
OFFICE DRAWER	6 (HIGH)	3 (HIGH)	18
STACK MAGS	3 (LOW)	9 (LOW)	27

From these two calculations, the magazine pile would precede the office drawer. Continue these calculations for each area that needs order.

CLEARING AGREEMENT

My agreement with myself is to complete the following by:

		Target	Completed
A.	Clean my living space totally.	________	________
B.	Clean my car thoroughly.	________	________
C.	Clean out my purse and/or wallet.	________	________
D.	Clean up my office, my kitchen drawers and my closet.	________	________
E.	Clean out and organize my personal files.	________	________
F.	Complete or get rid of unfinished stuff on my desk.	________	________
G.	Fix or get rid of anything that does not work.	________	________
H.	Throw or give away what I don't use or wear.	________	________
I.	Balance my checkbook.	________	________
J.	Pay my bills or make arrangements with my creditors.	________	________
K.	Organize my financial records.	________	________

L. Pay any taxes due, and put tax records in order. ______ ______

M. Collect and pay any money owed. ______ ______

N. Return anything borrowed and get back anything lent. ______ ______

O. Deliver any undelivered communications:

1. Letter to be written. ______ ______
2. Acknowledgements
   a. To be given ______ ______
   b. To be received ______ ______
3. Broken promises to be acknowledged. ______ ______
4. Any lies to be cleaned up. ______ ______
5. Anything hidden or held secret to be communicated. ______ ______

P. Resolve any broken agreements. ______ ______

Q. Resolve any upsets in my life (clean it up, or get rid of it). ______ ______

R. Handle or prepare a plan to handle anything which abuses my spirit, mental functioning and body, e.g. alcohol, smoking. ______ ______

S. Handle my primary relationships so that I have agreements or ground rules which support me. ______ ______

Bonus Exercise

This bonus exercise can give you a big boost toward dumping blocks to your created future. Take time to complete the sentences.

The goals in my life this past year were:

The goals I completed this year were:

The goals or projects I left incomplete that I intend to complete this year are:

The goals or projects I left incomplete that I have no intention of completing this year thus release are:

I acknowledge myself for:

I forgive myself for:

My highest goal for the coming year are:

NUTRIENTS TO HELP WITH FOCUS AND ORDER

Caffeine

Caffeine is a stimulant found in coffee, chocolate, and many carbonated beverages. It can help you become more alert, and thus able to process information more smoothly and quickly. Caffeine can be addictive. Over time your brain may develop a "need" for the drug in order to wake up. At this point, it probably isn't doing too much good.

Caffeine helps in small doses. It increases metabolism, and improves mental focus and energy. Tea's combo of caffeine and the L-theanine can improve alertness, reaction time, and memory. Caffeine and theobromine in chocolate are natural energy boosters. Always choose raw chocolate.

Omega-3

Omega-3 fatty acids in fish help improve brain function over time. Fish have high levels of both choline and omega-3 fatty acids; both linked to brain functionality. Choline, a B-vitamin, has a positive effect on the hippocampus.[6] Choose fatty fish such as wild salmon, tuna or anchovies, avocados, nuts or olive oil.

Watch your carbohydrate intake. Carbs are an essential part of nutrition, but given an overdose of carbs, our bodies shut down, creating sleepiness. Balancing protein, carb, and fat intake makes the body work most efficiently. Fruit and vegetables are actually carbohydrates, but are not nearly as dense as breads and pastas. Eating more fruits and vegetables and decreasing your intake of dense breads and pastas should help you focus for longer periods of time.

Blueberries

Blueberries can help protect the brain from oxidative stress and may reduce the effects of age-

---

6 In one experiment, rat pups given choline either in utero or within a few weeks showed life long memory enhancement. In another study, pregnant mothers were given either cod liver oil or corn oil throughout their pregnancies. Cod liver oil contains high levels of omega-3 fatty acids, and corn oil does not. The children of these mothers were given an IQ test at the age of 4, and the offspring of the mothers who were given cod liver oil scored significantly better than the corn oil group. Tests using choline with pregnant mothers produced similar results.

related conditions such as Alzheimer's disease or dementia. Studies also show that diets rich in blueberries significantly improved both the learning capacity and motor skills of aging rats, making them mentally equivalent to much younger rats.

Glucose

Sugar is your brain's preferred fuel source but not white table sugar! Your body metabolizes glucose from the sugars and carbs you eat. That's why a glass of something sweet to drink can offer a short-term boost to memory, thinking processes, and mental ability.

Previous research shows that a high serving of glucose may have a fast, short-term benefit on mental ability, especially where glucose metabolism isn't very efficient. But performance degrades quickly after peak dose. Too much, and your memory and focus can be impaired. Carbohydrates convert into glucose in the body, but carbs usually aren't available for the body to use for at least 2-4 hours, and proteins aren't available until after four hours.

Check the glycemic index of foods:
http://www.glycemicindex.com/

Studies show that children who eat breakfast tend to have better short-term memory than their peers who do not eat such meals. Kids who eat high-caloric breakfasts, however, have impaired concentration. The high-fat diet, may negatively impact alertness. In several studies, rats that were fed high-fat meals tended to have poorer learning and memory than counterparts who were fed more balanced diets.

Nuts and Chocolate

Nuts and seeds are good sources of the antioxidant vitamin E, associated with less cognitive decline over time. Raw chocolate has powerful antioxidant properties, and contains natural stimulants like caffeine, which can enhance focus and concentration. Note that regular chocolate loses most of it's antioxidant capacity due to processing; go for raw chocolate instead.

Sticking with foods high in choline and omega-3 fatty acids, and limiting your intake of dense carbs should help you become more alert and make learning easier for you. Use caffeine sparingly for a temporary boost, but don't make it a habit.

Magnesium

Magnesium was recommended for the Earth Element, and here it is again because of the role it plays in the ability to focus. Green vegetables such as spinach are good sources of magnesium because the center of the chlorophyll molecule contains magnesium. Some legumes such as beans and peas, nuts and seeds, and whole, unrefined grains are also good sources of magnesium.

Refined grains are low in magnesium. When white flour is processed, the magnesium-rich germ and bran are removed. Whole grain bread provides more magnesium than bread made from white refined flour. Tap water can be a source of magnesium and "hard" water contains more magnesium than "soft" water.

Check this link for Magnesium content of foods:
http://www.mgwater.com/content.shtml

Because of the importance of peak brain function to the Water Element, here are confirmed research findings:

- ☐ **L-glutamine** supports mental function.
- ☐ **N-acetyl Tyrosine** supports healthy cognitive and motor performance.
- ☐ **Gamma-amino butyric Acid** helps receptors in the brain regulate awareness, anxiety, muscle tension, and memory functions.
- ☐ **Choline** helps build and maintain brain cell membranes. It is also important for the production of healthy cell membranes.

- ☐ **Grape Skin Extract** has been shown in pre-clinical studies to support memory retention.
- ☐ **Bacopa Monnieri Extract** has been shown in clinical and pre-clinical studies to provide positive effects on acquisition and retention of memory.
- ☐ **Phosphatidylserine** has been shown in pre-clinical and clinical studies to support healthy brain functions and can improve age-associated deterioration of brain functions.
- ☐ **Ginkgo Biloba** is used to treat problems of concentration, dementia and a few studies show that Ginkgo can increase blood flow to the brain, but there are no conclusive studies that show it helps memory, focus or concentration.

Herbs to get in touch with the element of water:

Air is primarily wet and secondarily hot.
Fire is primarily hot and secondarily dry.
Earth is primarily dry and secondarily cold.
Water is primarily cold and secondarily wet.

Aloe, apple, apricot, birch, blackberry, chamomile, cherry, comfrey, daffodil, daisy, elder, foxglove, heather, iris, jasmine, lemon, lilac, myrrh, orris, peach, plum, poppy, raspberry, rose, sandalwood, strawberry, tansy, thyme, vanilla, violet, willow. They have all been associated with enhancing the Water element. Go to the counter, smell them all and chose one you like.

Drinking water keeps your blood oxygenated and prevents dehydration, which causes fatigue and impairs concentration.

During your work in the Water Element, get in touch with the element of water. Walk in the rain or swim in the ocean. Soak in a tub with your favorite herbs.

Water is the element of wisdom. How about divination[7] with a bowl of water? Add blue food coloring, light a candle, toss some sandalwood oil on the water surface, gaze into the water and see if images appear.

To the west of your home or apartment, place a big bowl of water with floating rose petals. Open the windows and doors on the west side, and facing west, invite the spirit of Water to commune with you. I bet it's even better on a rainy day.

---

7 http://en.wikipedia.org/wiki/Divination

FOUR ELEMENTS JOURNAL

ELEMENT THREE: AIR

Face the yellow/orange element of air. Circle your eyes counter clockwise through all three spirals. Voice your intention. "Thank you Air for energy and balance."

Air is a universal power with fundamental centrality to life. The terms aspire, inspire, perspire and spirit are all derived from the Latin *spirare*. According to Plato, air is hot and wet. Blood was the humor identified with air; both were hot and wet. Other associations with air were the season of spring, with its qualities of heat and moisture and a sanguine temperament. Childhood, sunrise, the colors yellow and white, and qualities of mind, intellect, study, consciousness and communications. The exercises in this Part III of your Journal improve the flow and balance of energy in your life.

Developing the qualities of Air requires gating the energy leaving and entering your physical and mental space. Your first workout is the Sphere of Availability.

SPHERE OF AVAILABILITY

Write 4-5 things you have or do inside the Sphere above, and 4-5 things you would *like to do and have, but don't,* outside the sphere.

Whatever lies outside the sphere is outside your comfort zone and thus your risk area. Our work will be to get whatever you choose from outside the sphere into a place inside the sphere. You believe that whatever is outside your comfort zone is currently unattainable to you. For example, you have a rented place east of town (inside the circle), but you want to live in a trendy loft downtown (outside the circle). You earn $85,000 per year (inside the circle) and want $855,000 per year (outside). You are among the top 100 performers (inside) in your company and you want to be in the top 5 (outside). You get the idea.

Make a list of the items you wrote down inside the sphere. You are comfortable with these. There is no threat or growth here.

1.
2.
3.
4.
5.

Make a list of the items you wrote down outside the sphere. You are uncomfortable with these. There is threat and growth here.

1.
2.
3.
4.
5.

Completing this exercise is an eye opener. As you look at what you have written, try to think why these items are where they are. **You have made choices to put them there**. Below are five quick starts to getting them inside your circle – your new belief system.

Imagine that you have no fears, no limits. Create the perfect life for yourself. Try to fill in something for each blank.

The bad habits I have let go are ___________,
____________, __________.

New personality traits I have developed are _________,
__________, _________

My dream home has is located in ________________ and I feel _________________ in it.

I wear ___________, ____________, and ____________ clothes.

I am earning _______________ per year, and have a net worth of ________________.

I am maintaining my ideal weight of _____ lbs.

I am healing my family communications by ___________, ____________, ______________.

I am improving my work environment by ______________ and ________________.

My new hobbies include ______________, ____________, and ________________.

To become fit I am ________, __________, and ___________.

Two new skills I am learning for my work include ___________ and ____________,

I am with my ideal soul mate who is ________, __________, and __________.

To induce calm in my life I am _________, _________, and ___________.

New habits I have are ______________, _____________, and ______________

I am serving my community by ___________, _______________, and _________________

Others now describe me as ____________,
____________, and ______________

The people I have met, and stay in touch with, are
________ and ___________.

Write out the last couple of pages and keep them with you – read every day without fail.

Vanquishing Mental Viruses

There are predictable styles of thinking that can create a constant energy leak. They are no-win approaches to life, and never work to get you want you want. That's why they call them mental viruses, and they are difficult to treat.

With any of these mental viruses, it will be impossible for you to sustain the success you want:

____ **1. Trying to be happy?** What do you do in the pursuit of happiness rather than accomplishing other goals? Stop trying to be happy and doing things specifically to be 'happy.' Happiness is a by-product of giving, loving and pursuing a worthwhile goal.[8]

____ **2. Never being content with what you have;** always wanting what you don't have? End each

8 Check my book Positive Spin, which outlines what it really takes to be happy.

day with a Gratitude List. Make a mental or physical note of five qualities, people, or things in your life for which you are grateful.

____ **3. Comparing yourself to others?** Rather than comparing yourself, which is an impossible unrewarding trip, compare yourself with your own progress. Are you a percentage ahead now in any area than you were last year? Last month? That is excellent. You are doing well. It is good enough.

HOW TO LEARN OPTIMISM

Pessimism expends more energy than optimism because it requires additional emotional action. When you see the worst, then your mental and physical energy start to get bound up in preparing for the worst. Looking for the best doesn't result in additional stress.

This is how to switch from pessimism to optimism. After both positive and negative outcomes, optimists and pessimists ask the same questions, but they give different answers.

They both ask these questions:

1. **Who caused this?**
2. **Is that just the way that person is, or is it an exception?**

3. Is this always the way it's going to be, or just this time?

Supposing Mike is an optimist, and John is a pessimist. They both want to leave their jobs and start insurance careers. They both pass the insurance exam. The answers they give to the three questions are in italics:

Mike's 3 answers (optimist):

1. Who caused this? "I caused this. This was due to my hard work." (success is internal)

2. Is that just the way that person is, or is it an exception? "All of me, I'm a pretty smart person." (global thinking)

3. Is this always the way it's going to be, or just this time? "That's just like me; passing is something I usually do." (success is stable)

John's 3 answers (pessimist):

1. Who caused this?

"Just got lucky I guess. Easy exam." (success is external: the easy exam caused the passing)

2. Is that just the way that person is, or is it an exception? "I just got lucky this time ... just with this exam."

3. Is this always the way it's going to be, or just this time? "That's really not like me! I can't expect that to happen again (this thing happened just once, usually it doesn't)."

What happens if they both failed the exam?

Mike's 3 answers (optimist):

1. Who caused this? "The exam was very hard." (failure is external) or "I didn't study enough."

2. Is that just the way that person is, or is it an exception? "Usually I do fine but that time I got bad luck, I guess or I just didn't study enough. I do well in other things. Next time I'll pass." (failure specific, not all of me)

3. Is this always the way it's going to be, or just this time? "That's really not like me! Usually I do well." (failure unstable, changing)

John's 3 answers (pessimist):

1. Who caused this?
"I blew it." (failure is internal)

2. Is that just the way that person is, or is it an exception? "I'm just a screw up!" (global, all of him failed).

3. Is this always the way it's going to be, or just this time? "I never do well at anything." (stable, unchanging).

Persons who feel helpless, and Pessimists, think negative events are Internal Stable & Global. Mastery-oriented persons and Optimists think negative events are External, Changing & Specific and when events are positive, it's just the reverse. That doesn't mean that optimists aren't able to self-examine and learn from their experiences. But their thinking allows them to keep moving rather than being stuck. Which would you rather be?

Switching to Optimism

Review the differences between optimistic and pessimistic thinking. Then listen for your reactions to both positive and negative events. Compare your reactions to the examples above. The optimist's examples provide a script for you to follow when either positive or negative things happen to you. If you change your script, you will change your life and what you are creating in it.

You are the only one who can change this thinking. If you don't change your thinking, what you attract to your life won't change either. If you do change it, everything will change.

BURNOUT

LEVEL 1: GREEN ZONE (SAFE)

☐ I work in the evenings, even when I don't have to.

☐ I wish I had a week that others didn't, just to catch up.

☐ I don't have much time for myself, or family and friends.

☐ It seems that every minute of every day is scheduled.

☐ I feel More scattered, sometimes overwhelmed.

☐ I often feel exhausted – even early in the week.

___TOTAL

LEVEL 2: YELLOW ZONE (WARNING)

☐ I know I should exercise more, but I just don't get to it.

☐ I can't remember the last time I was able to find the time to take a day off to do something fun, just for me.

☐ I can't remember the last time I read and finished a book that I was reading just for pleasure.

☐ I wish I had more time for some outside interests and hobbies, but I simply don't.

☐ My family says they need more time or attention from me and I tell them: "Later, when the (crunch) is over."

___ TOTAL

LEVEL 3: RED ZONE (DANGER)

☐ I've missed several of my family's important events because of work commitments.

☐ Sometimes I feel as though I've lost sight of who I am and why I chose this job/career.

☐ My neck and/or shoulders bother me more. I'm getting more colds and they last longer.

☐ My eye twitches.

☐ Life's no fun any more. I feel caught.

___ TOTAL

If your score is between 4-7, you are still safe. But look through the statements you checked and see if there is an alternate. You might want to call a dead zone in the afternoon and stop working. Make sure you keep your friends and hobbies.

If your score is over seven (7), consider the following:

a. List everything you do in a given day.

b. Rank each from 0-100 in long-term consistency with what you say is important, and with its pay-off.

c. Drop the bottom third of the list.

d. Ink in dates with children, spouse or friends, favorite exercise, a hobby.

It's not too late. Do something about it now.

PATIENCE

Here's a challenge for you. This is an assessment following up on Chapter Seven of the *Four Elements.*

Lack of patience can result from a belief that the world should center around you and not interfere with your comings and goings. People should do things your way because, well, you know better. If everyone did what they were supposed to do, the world would be a better place and you would be much happier.

If you can see the futility of this thinking, you're half way there. The other half is to notice times when you're impatient and either recite the serenity prayer mentioned earlier, or for a quick fix, take a glance at this card. Let it go. Not worth it. Not your road. It will work out. Really.

STOP SCREAMING AT THE STOPLIGHT

Respond with either 2 (often),1 (sometimes), or 0 (never) according to how true the statements are for you. Then add up your score.

2 Often 1 Sometimes 0 Rarely or Never

_____1. I can get irritated with slow elevators and red traffic lights.
_____2. I tend to hurry slower people and finish their sentences.
_____3. I admit it, I get annoyed by certain kinds of people.
_____4. The idiots driving on the highway should be eaten by lions.
_____5. I can get upset with my kids when they aren't DOING anything productive.
_____6. I wish people would get to the point.
_____7. I hate having to wait in line, in fact, I sometimes have little tantrums.

________Your Score /14

MORE HELP WITH ENERGY AND BALANCE

Air Terms: aspire, inspire, hot, wet, spring, masculine, childhood, sunrise, south. Air is attributed to the East and to the Mind.

These circles represent continuous movement of air, but in balance. Since Air rises, it's natural to think of Air as arising out of Spirit. A circle is a symbol for Spirit, but also a symbol of infinity, unity and community. We use the color of dark yellow, or orange.

Invocation of the Element of Air.

State your morning purpose in the form of: "I invoke you to _____" and fill in the blank. This intention is related to the World of Air, the World of the Mind. Your intention can be to remove mental confusion, improve mental concentration or attention, improve memory or memory recall, expand your mind, improve your attitude.

The World of Air is your mind, your thoughts and ideas, imagination, and memory. Choose any of these things as your purpose as you meditate. Gaze at the small circles and trace each of them in a clockwise direction in the morning and counterclockwise in the evening. Concentrate on those motions as you state your gratitude for the expression of that element for that day. You can place the intention in your Spirit box in the morning and leave it there, taking it out at night when you can. Give thanks for whatever part of the Air Element was expressed that day. With the rising of a new sun, intentions get to be expressed anew so don't worry about leaving intentions in too long.

Practice the Air element every morning for 7-10 days and see how it goes. Use as much time as you need, and come back to it whenever you need.

The Element of Air is associated with sound–any kind of sound including psychic or disincarnate voices. When developing the Air Element, banish all unwanted voices and sounds.

EXERCISE

If you need more energy, this is where to start. Start small. Even a 10-minute walk is energizing, and the benefits go up with frequency. Regular exercise can boost mood and trigger physiological changes that make more energy available throughout the day. Data from 4,641 women ages 40-65, found a strong link between depression and lower physical activity levels, and a higher calorie intake.

FOOD AND ENERGY

Food can boost energy three ways: by giving you enough calories, by delivering stimulants like caffeine, and by pushing your metabolism to burn fuel more efficiently. For mood boosts, the best foods are those that stabilize blood sugar and trigger certain brain chemicals such as serotonin.

Carbs are good for boosting energy and mood. They're the body's preferred source of fuel, and they raise serotonin levels. The connection between carbohydrates and mood is all about tryptophan, a nonessential amino acid. As more tryptophan enters the brain, more serotonin is synthesized, and mood improves. Serotonin, known as a mood regulator, is made naturally in the brain from tryptophan with some help from the B vitamins. Foods thought to increase serotonin levels in the brain include fish and vitamin D.

Here's the catch: While tryptophan is found in almost all protein-rich foods, other amino acids are better at passing from the bloodstream into the brain. So you can boost your tryptophan levels by eating more carbs; they help cut down the competition for tryptophan, so more of it can enter the brain. Make smart carb choices like whole grains, fruits, vegetables, and legumes, which also contribute important nutrients and fiber.

Avoid sweets, because they cause blood sugar to spike up and and plummet down, which makes you tired and moody.

Magnesium and Selenium

Almonds, hazelnuts and cashews contain lots of protein, and they also contain magnesium, a mineral that helps convert sugar into energy. Brazil nuts add selenium, which may be a natural mood booster. Selenium is also in smaller amounts in meats, seafood, beans, and whole grains. Magnesium deficiency can drain energy! Magnesium is also found in whole grains, especially bran cereals, and in some types of fish, including halibut, bread, brown rice, and cereal. The body absorbs whole grains more slowly.

Caffeine

Small doses of caffeine were recommended for your Water Element Work. Caffeine helps in *small* doses. It increases metabolism, and improves mental focus and energy. Tea's combo of caffeine and the L-theanine can improve alertness, reaction time, and memory. Caffeine and theobromine in chocolate are natural energy boosters.

Eat Breakfast. Eat Frequent Meals.

People who eat breakfast every morning have more energy and are in a better mood all day.

Omega-3 polyunsaturated fatty acids (fatty fish, flaxseed, and walnuts) may help protect against depression and keep energy higher. This makes sense physiologically; Omega-3s affect neurotransmitter pathways in the brain.

Foods rich in selenium are foods we should be eating anyway such as: Seafood (oysters, clams, sardines, crab, saltwater fish and freshwater fish), nuts and seeds (particularly Brazil nuts), lean meat (lean pork and beef, skinless chicken and turkey), whole grains (whole-grain pasta, brown rice, oatmeal, etc.), beans/legumes, low-fat dairy products.

Herbs that connect with the element of air.

Acacia, Almond, Aspen, Bittersweet, Bodhi, Brazil nut, Broom, Caraway, Clover, Dandelion, Goldenrod, Hazel, Hops, Lavender, Maple, Marjoram, Mistletoe, Mulberry, Pecan, Pine.

Grab a fistful of any one of these in flake form. Sit outside on a windy day, when the wind is blowing from the east. Hold the powdered herb in your hand and let the wind take it away as you release wishes and dreams, or anything else you'd like the wind to know. Listen, see if anything is revealed.

Don't wait for Christmas. Hang mistletoe at any openings of your house that face east and open windows or doors if the climate is right, and let the wind through your house while you're inside.

Hang almonds from wind chimes with yellow string or cord, facing east try divination described elsewhere.

Essential Oils for Energy

Oils with spicy or citrus scents are the best at increasing energy. Lime oil is a good energizer and blends well with basil, which helps stimulate as well. Ginger is invigorating–try it with grapefruit.

Low Temperature Dehydrated (Dried) Coconut

How coconut is prepared is important. This is the best way: coconuts are removed from the shells, washed in pure, filtered water (no chlorine). The coconut is then shredded and slowly dehydrated at no more than 98.6° F (37° C).

Most shredded, dried coconut available online and in health food stores is actually desiccated coconut. Chlorinated water is used to clean and sterilize the coconuts once they are opened and peeled. The coconut meat is grated, often lightly pressed to remove some of the milk (moisture) and then it is dried in huge ovens at temperatures between 170°-180° F (76°-82° C). Coconut sold in grocery stores is made from this dessicated coconut by soaking it in corn syrup, propylene glycol and sodium metabisulfate to preserve it. There is a huge difference between raw dehydrated coconut and most store-bought sweetened coconut flakes.

Coconut is highly nutritious and rich in fiber, vitamins, and minerals, classified as a 'functional food' because it provides so many health benefits beyond its nutritional content. Coconut oil possesses healing properties far beyond that of any other dietary oil, and is extensively used in traditional medicine among Asian and Pacific populations. Pacific Islanders consider coconut oil to be the cure for all illness, and the coconut palm is so highly valued by them as both a source of food and medicine that it is called "The Tree of Life."

FOUR ELEMENTS JOURNAL

ELEMENT FOUR: FIRE

Put your intention in your own words, and imagine a flaming red fire reaching outwards and upwards, visualize it as clearly as you can, let your eyes begin at the base and move upwards, seeing your intention rise with the fire, and repeat this as long as you wish. Once is fine, but you can repeat 3-5 times. Feel it's heat, almost bring red near it's base.

At the end of the day, "Thank you Fire for .... and now I release ...."

Fire is associated with energy, assertiveness, and passion. In one Greek myth, Prometheus stole fire from the gods to protect helpless humans. In ancient Greek medicine, yellow bile was the humor identified with fire; both were hot and dry as in the 'choleric' temperament.[9] Other attributions include: the season of summer, the masculine, and the east.

Fire is an active force that has the passion to create and animate. Fire in many ancient cultures and myths has been known to purify the land with the flames of destruction, however, it is also capable of the renewal of life through the warmth of those flames.

Fire contains both Air and Water, so we combine the world of thoughts (Air) and emotions (Water). Fire is also the Element of courage, passion, drive, force, energy, enthusiasm–all things outgoing, facing upward, outwards and in expansion.

The Element of Fire is associated with sight, any form of visual aid including their physical body when incarnate here on Earth. When banishing Fire also banish all unwanted visions of every kind.

Fire represents creativity and passion; an active force that creates and animates and renews. In ancient Greek medicine, yellow bile was the humor identified with fire; both were hot and dry. Summer; the masculine, the east, the Sun.

---

9 Heraclitus (c.535BCE–c.475BCE) considered fire to be the most fundamental of all elements, giving rise to the other three elements: "All things are an interchange for fire, and fire for all things, just like goods for gold and gold for goods".

Look fear straight in the eyes: Act despite the fear. You can't take away the fear, so "feel the fear and do it anyway."

Remember the Excuses exercise from Page 14 of this Journal? This is a similar exercise. Run through answers to these questions. The answers you give can help spur you to action if you enter what it would take to create an answer that would reflect your transformed self.

Is your career as rewarding and meaningful as you'd like? If not, what would it take to create that?

Are you financially secure? If not, what would it take to create that?

Are your relationships healthy and satisfying? If not, what would it take to create that?

Are you living up to your potential? If not, what would it take to create that?

Is your spirit free? If not, what would it take to create that?

Are there dreams that you used to have that you've given up? If not, what would it take to re-create them?

Are you as happy as you'd wished you could be? If not, what would it take to create that?

Are your friends as loving as you wish? If not, what would it take to create that?

Money

Money is just energy, and follows the same rules as other forms of energy. It's time to stop wasting *your* energy worrying about it. Hopefully, you are following the guidelines in Chapter 12 of your *Four Elements* Book. The following practices will take you deeper into your understanding of your relationship with money so that you can finally be in control of this important form of energy in your life.

Below are several assignments, with further explanations written in italics below the space that is provided for your answers.

1. How much money do you want, and how would it make you feel if you had it?

How you can make yourself feel that way before you get more money? Happiness leads to money, money does not lead to happiness.

2. Draw a picture of a wealthy person and picture his or her living space and demeanor. Draw a picture of a poor person and picture his or her living space and demeanor.

The wealthy person might have space, freedom, and ease of movement. The poor person's world might be cluttered, restricted, and uncomfortable. Fix your current surroundings now to be closer to your image of wealth. Surely, you can declutter, create space, and make part of your world easier. Start with what you can control now.

3. How do you feel about wealthy people? How do you feel about money? What words did you learn about money? The root of all evil?[10] How do you feel about poor people? Do you have a romantic image of creativity and poverty?

You might have a hidden disdain or fear of wealthy people, or consider them selfish or shallow. If so, it will be hard to draw wealth to yourself because you cannot tolerate seeing yourself as selfish or shallow. There is no relationship between creativity and poverty; many prolific artists were wealthy.

Tim. 6:10: "For the love of money placed before the love of God is the root of all kinds of evil."The love of money for itself is the critical factor. If money is used for good, then it is in God's will that you be blessed with an abundance of it.

Did anything new come up about your relationship with money? Can you make the decision to change some of your perceptions?

INCREASING THE FIRE ELEMENT

Phenylalanine

Phenylalanine is an essential amino acid available in three chemical forms: L-phenylalanine (the natural form found in proteins throughout the body), D-phenylalanine (synthesized in lab), and DL-phenylalanine, a combination.

The body converts phenylalanine into tyrosine, an amino acid essential for making brain chemicals including dopamine, norepinephrine, and thyroid hormones. Symptoms of phenylalanine deficiency include confusion, lack of energy, depression, decreased alertness, decreased memory, and diminished appetite.

Dopamine: Natural ways to Increase Dopamine

Dopamine is an excitatory and inhibitory neurotransmitter, depending on the dopamine receptor it binds to, comes from the amino acid tyrosine. Dopamine is the precursor to norepinephrine and epinephrine, all catecholamines. Dopamine plays a large role in the pleasure/reward pathway (addiction and thrills), memory, and motor control. Dopamine, like norepinephrine and epinephrine, is stored in vesicles in the axon terminal.

Symptoms of Dopamine Deficiency. Low dopamine levels are associated with depression, loss of motor control, loss of satisfaction, addictions, cravings, compulsions, low sex drive, poor attention and focus. When dopamine levels are elevated (too high) symptoms may manifest in anxiety, paranoia, or hyperactivity.

Dopamine levels are depleted by stress, certain antidepressants, drug use, poor nutrition, and poor sleep. Alcohol, caffeine, and sugar all seem to decrease dopamine activity in the brain.

Foods that increase Dopamine. Food sources of dopamine increasing tyrosine include almonds, avocados, bananas, dairy products, lima beans, pumpkin seeds, and sesame seeds.

Dopamine is easily oxidized; foods rich in antioxidants such as fruits and vegetables may help protect dopamine-using neurons from free radical damage. Foods such as sugar, saturated fats, cholesterol, and refined foods interfere with proper brain function, and can reduce dopamine. Consumption of saturated fats and cholesterol should also be reduced because they can clog the arteries to the brain, heart, and other organs.

Caffeine should be avoided by persons with depression. Caffeine is a stimulant which initially speeds up neurotransmission, raises the amount of serotonin, and temporarily elevates mood.

Dopamine precursors are specific amino acids that our brains use to manufacture dopamine. Neurotransmitters are frequently not supplied in great enough levels by our diet or in the way our brain best utilizes them. As stress further depletes supplies it is difficult, if not impossible, for the brain to restore necessary amounts to proper levels.

Aromatherapy for Fire Element

For grounding and courageous decision-making: Try lemon, cedarwood, & bergamot, Thyme, Ylang Ylang and other pure essential oils.

> "With courage you will dare to take risks, have the strength to be compassionate, and the wisdom to be humble. Courage is the foundation of integrity."
> Keshavan Nair

TAKE RISKS – NOT CHANCES!

YOUR RISK ANALYSIS

Three Risk (+) Elements increase risk safety:

a. information

b. time

c. control.

INFORMATION

* How much do you really know about this situation?
* Do you need to investigate more?
* Should you ask for guidance, read more, ask questions of those who have taken your risk?
* Have you practiced, rehearsed and sampled what you're getting into?

Think about the specific risk you would like to take now. Rate the information you have about this risk, placing the number in the space above to the left of "Information."

_____ **Information:**

0 None at all, I have no info, not a clue

10 I have complete information, I know everything there is to know.

Any arbitrary number from 0-10 is fine, depending on how you rate it.

TIME

* Are you pressured to take action or do you have time to prepare?

* Can you extend the decision deadline and give yourself some room, or is there no choice here?

Think now about the specific risk you would like to take, and rate the time you have, placing the number in the space above to the left of "Time."

_____ **Time:**

0 None, I have no time, I have to move now

10 I have all the time I want; I didn't wait till things got really bad.

CONTROL

* Have you gathered all the resources you can?
* Who can you ask for for help?
* Have you sought support and found those who have been through it and asked them to guide you?
* Are all the persons who will be affected by the risk on your side: have you taken the time to persuade, influence, befriend these people, or will they sabotage your risk?
* Who makes the decisions along the way. Is it just you, or do other important others make some of the decisions?

Think now about the specific risk you would like to take, and rate the control you have, placing the number in the space above to the left of "Control."

_____ **Control:**

0 None, I have no control, I make none of the decisions, I have built up no support or resources

10 I have all the support I want; I make all the decisions concerning this risk

In the boxes to the left of each rating, you now have 3 scores representing the certainty of your risk represented by the information, time and control you have. Add these up and you'll get a number between 0 and 30.

Total Time+Risk+Control = _______ (A)

PART B: RISK NEGATIVES

There are three components to the risk itself:
a. the impact
b. scope of the potential loss
c. probability that there will be a loss at all.

IMPACT

* How severe will the loss be?
* How much will the loss affect my life?
* Supposing I blow it, what's the the worst thing that would happen?

Now rate the impact the potential loss from this risk will have and enter the number in the space to the left of "Impact."

_____ **Impact:**

0 None, no impact, not serious, who cares?

10 Severe impact, it would be serious.

SCOPE

* What is the scope of the loss? How big will it be?
* How many people will know?
* How much will it spread out?

Now rate the scope the potential loss from this risk will have and enter the number in the space to the left of "Scope."

_____ **Scope:**

0 None at all, no spread at all. No-one will know or be affected.

10 There is a large fall out. Lots of people will be affected.

CHANCE

* What's the chance or probability of loss?
* How many similar risks have ended successfully?
* What are the statistics for your risk? Be objective here, because it's one of the first elements of risk we ignore when our emotions are involved or when we become too invested in a risk.

Now rate the chance or probability of loss from this risk and enter the number in the space to the left of "Chance of Loss."

_____ **Chance**

0 None, no chance of loss

10 This is a sure mess up, there's no way this has ever worked.

In the spaces to the left of each rating, you have three scores representing the loss potential represented by the impact of loss, scope of loss, and chance of loss. Add these up and you'll get a number between zero and 30.

Total Impact+Scope+Probability = _______ (B)
Subtract your total for B from your total for A to get your risk safety score, providing either a red, amber, or green light.

______ A - _____ B = ________ Risk Score

Scores can range from +30 to -30. The lower the score, the more risky the choice; that is, the more probability of loss. If your score is between -30 and -15 it is a definite no-go until you increase A and decrease B.

Between -15 and +15, proceed cautiously. Between +15 and +30, you're gold! If you really want this, you're ready! Go!

Get the Risk Forces on your side: Information, Time and Control. Before my first flight across Africa, I learned from my score that I needed more more information, and that I was pressured for time. My risk ended up being safe, but it might not have been if I had not applied a calculated approach.

In new business and personal ventures, the same calculations work. Use it for any risk you would like to take, and after you have used it a few times, the questions will become automatic, and you will find that you are taking risks instead of chances, and taking more risks as well.

THE IBI SCALE - SHORT FORM

Agree	Disagree		Score	Statement
____	____	•	____	1. It is important to me that others approve of me.
____	____	•	____	2. I hate to fail at anything.
____	____	•	____	3. People who do wrong deserve what they get.
____	____	••	____	4. I usually accept what happens philosophically.
____	____	••	____	5. If a person wants to, s/he can be happy under almost any circumstances.
____	____	•	____	6. I have a fear of some things that often bothers me.
____	____	•	____	7. I usually put off important decisions.
____	____	•	____	8. Everyone needs someone s/he can depend on for help and advice.
____	____	•	____	9. "A zebra can not change his/her stripes."
____	____	•	____	10. I prefer quiet leisure above all things.
____	____	••	____	11. I like the respect of others, but I don't have to have it.
____	____	•	____	12. I avoid things I cannot do well.
____	____	•	____	13. Too many evil persons escape the punishment they deserve.
____	____	••	____	14. Frustrations do not upset me.
____	____	••	____	15. People are disturbed not by situations but by the view they take of them.
____	____	••	____	16. I feel little anxiety over unexpected dangers or future events.
____	____	••	____	17. I try to go ahead and get irksome tasks behind me when they come up.
____	____	•	____	18. I try to consult an authority on important decisions.
____	____	•	____	19. It is almost impossible to overcome the influences of the past.
____	____	••	____	20. I like to have a lot of irons in the fire.

Agree	Disagree		Score	Statement
____	____	•	____	21. I want everyone to like me.
____	____	••	____	22. I don't mind competing in activities in which others are better than I.
____	____	•	____	23. Those who do wrong deserve to be blamed.
____	____	•	____	24. Things should be different from the way they are.
____	____	••	____	25. I cause my own moods.
____	____	•	____	26. I often can't get my mind off some concern.
____	____	•	____	27. I avoid facing my problems.
____	____	•	____	28. People need a source of strength outside themselves.
____	____	••	____	29. Just because something once strongly affected your life doesn't mean it need do so now.
____	____	••	____	30. I'm most fulfilled when I have lots to do.
____	____	••	____	31. I can like myself even when many others don't.
____	____	••	____	32. I like to succeed at something, but I don't feel I have to.
____	____	•	____	33. Immorality should be strongly punished.
____	____	•	____	34. I often get disturbed over situations I don't like.
____	____	••	____	35. People who are miserable have usually made themselves that way.
____	____	••	____	36. If I can't keep something from happening, I don't worry about it.
____	____	••	____	37. I usually make decisions as promptly as I can.
____	____	•	____	38. There are certain people that I depend on greatly.
____	____	••	____	39. People overvalue the influence of the past.
____	____	••	____	40. I most enjoy throwing myself into a creative project.

SCORING

ADD SINGLE DOT ITEMS: If the item has one dot [•] and you checked the "agree" box, give yourself 1 [one] point in the space provided next to the statement.

ADD DOUBLE DOT ITEMS: If the item has two dots [••] and you checked the "disagree" box, give yourself a point in the space provided next to the statement.

Add up your points for the following items:

1, 11, 21, 31	A= Total_______
2, 12, 22, 32	B= Total_______
3, 13, 23, 33	C= Total_______
4, 14, 24, 34	D= Total_______
5, 15, 25, 35	E= Total_______
6, 16, 26, 36	F= Total_______
7, 17, 27, 37	G= Total_______
8, 18, 28, 38	H= Total_______
9, 19, 29, 39,	I= Total_______
10, 20, 30, 40	J= Total_______

Results:[11]

A= The higher the total, the greater your agreement with the irrational idea that it is an absolute necessity for an adult to have love and approval from peers, family and friends.

This blocks you when you try to please others too much, or do things simply because if you do you, you fear others will be disappointed or angry with you. Have the courage throughout this program to question this belief (it is not true, we do not need love and approval – we like it, but do not need it). You might be blocked in what YOU need to do.

B= The higher the total, the greater your agreement with the irrational idea that you must be unfailingly competent and almost perfect in all you undertake.

This is high enough to prevent you from doing anything unless it's perfect and of course - it never is at first. So you might be avoiding doing certain things altogether? And you are probably very hard on yourself, beat yourself when you don't do well. It is really hard to be as successful as you want to be if you keep this up. You must tolerate mistakes, not doing well, and accept these and stop getting mad at yourself.

C= The higher the total, the greater your agreement with the irrational idea that certain people are evil, wicked and villainous, and should be punished.

---

11 These are suggestions only. One of the strengths of the IBI is that it can be used by the motivated layperson to discover hindering beliefs. If the interpretation of any of these scores is troublesome or confusing, please call in to a teleseminar that covers the Inventory (announced in advance), or send me an email and I will respond.

This score might have more to do with global terrorism rather than personal blocks. But if there is any resentment toward anyone in your life, it is not helping you to stay attached to this. "The best revenge is living well."

D= The higher the total, the greater your agreement with the irrational idea that it is horrible when things are not the way you would like them to be.

This belief takes a fairly high toll on us, things must be a certain way or it is very upsetting. Things are the way we want them to be very rarely. We aim toward a goal, we get close sometimes. And it is hard to let go of control. We care very much about it being right. Someone once said "There are many paths to the palace of wisdom." Start letting go. Relax. Easier said than done.

E= The higher the total, the greater your agreement with the irrational idea that external events cause most human misery- people simply react as events trigger their emotions.

F= The higher the total, the greater your agreement with the irrational idea that you should feel fear or anxiety about anything that is unknown, uncertain or potentially dangerous.

Rethink the unknown as **exciting** rather than **dangerous.** It's the same emotion, just a different label. You will be safe.

G= The higher the total, the greater your agreement with the irrational idea that it is easier to avoid than to face life difficulties and responsibilities.

Your score was somewhat higher than it should be for an entrepreneur! Is there a slight tendency to avoid facing tough interactions, or conflict maybe? Or wanting to escape the drudgery that goes along with success? Re-think this one!!

H= The higher the total, the greater your agreement with the irrational idea that you need something other or stronger or greater than yourself to rely on.
This is a familiar belief of many women, that we need to rely on experts, or that we are not ready, or that we are not enough on our own. Repeat often "I am enough, I have enough, I do enough."

I= The higher the total, the greater your agreement with the irrational idea that the past has a lot to do with determining the present.

J= The higher the total, the greater your agreement with the irrational idea that happiness can be achieved by in action, passivity and endless leisure.
Success comes from hard work, we have to choose leisure or success. This work is often joyful, often exciting, but it is hard in that we need to keep focused, put in the hours, put in the effort. Happiness comes from focused work toward a goal. No other way. Read Scott Peck's classic: *The Road Less Travelled.*

SAMPLE BUSINESS PLAN

OBJECTIVES

NAME: ______________________________

My Core Purpose:

My Expertise:

20__ Optimistic Goal $ ______
20__ Realistic Goal $ ______

Quarter 1 January 1 to March 31 _____________
Quarter 2 April 1 to June 30 _____________
Quarter 3 July 1 September 30 _____________
Quarter 4 October 1 to December 31 _____________
TOTAL _____________

January 1 to March 31, 20__ Goal Statements:

1. ______________________________ . I will do that by:
- **a. ______________________________**
- **b. ______________________________**
- **d. ______________________________**

2. ______________________________ . I will do that by:
- **a. ______________________________**
- **b. ______________________________**
- **d. ______________________________**

3. ______________________________ . I will do that by:

a. ______________________________
b. ______________________________
d. ______________________________

Continue for each quarter.

Follow the suggestions for Element Two goal work on page 95 in your Four Elements text.

Register for the Four Elements System online. As a reader, you are eligible to attend group teleseminars at no extra charge! When you register, watch for announcements that will be sent to you.

Requests for speaking engagements should be made through your favorite Speakers Bureau, or request information through the website www.lapp.com.

Orders for books or other resources and materials may be made through www.lapp.com. Those pertaining to the Four Elements System can be accessed through http://www.lapp.com/Lapp/Four_Elements.html. SIgn up for complimentary teleseminars at Four Elements on www.lapp.com. I look forward to meeting you!